CALIFORNIA
SIERRA NEVADA
JOHN FIELDER

Photography and Words
by John Fielder

California Littlebooks

Westcliffe Publishers, Inc. Englewood, Colorado

First frontispiece: The Alabama Hills with Mt.
Whitney behind, Inyo County

Second frontispiece: Alpine tarn at sunset, below
Piute Pass

Third frontispiece: Shooting-star, cinquefoil, and
Indian paintbrush wildflowers, North Fork Big
Pine Creek

Opposite: Clyde Minaret reflects into an alpine
tarn, Ansel Adams Wilderness

International Standard Book Number:
ISBN 0-942394-25-9
Library of Congress Catalogue Card Number:
86-050067
Copyright: John Fielder, 1986
Designer: Gerald Miller Simpson/Denver
Typographer: Edward A. Nies
Printer: Dai Nippon Printing Company, Ltd.
               Tokyo, Japan
Publisher: Westcliffe Publishers, Inc.
               P.O. Box 1261
               Englewood, Colorado 80150-1261

PREFACE

I began photographing California when the need grew from within to see and experience new landscapes. Most of my career as a nature photographer had been occupied up to this point exploring and photographing the alpine domains of Colorado. I suppose I could always be happy in Colorado, but that same urge that drives me to seek the unknown around the bend in the trail drove me to see California.

In part I went to California because it offered so many new landforms to which I had not previously been exposed. The Pacific Ocean and the deserts of southern and eastern California I knew would challenge my creativity with the camera. It is not easy to make good images on film of subjects that you don't understand or for which you don't have emotion.

One needs to spend time just walking and exploring, experiencing the different types of weather and the resulting conditions of light and their visual effects on the land. One needs to see new places throughout the seasons in order to realize the total character of the land. Therefore, I spent many months trying to photograph the wonderful beaches and stark deserts of California, but only after about a year did I begin to see emotion and a sense for the unusual in my work.

The pattern was a bit different, though, when I began to photograph the Sierra Nevada Mountains. I had spent much of my life experiencing the wild alpine domains of Colorado, and I felt I knew much about alpine weather and the resulting conditions of light that are so important to the photographer. I believed I was prepared immediately upon my first view of the Sierras to accurately record their character on film.

I was wrong. Though there are many similarities between the Rockies of Colorado and the Sierra Nevada of California, there are many dramatic differences. The weather patterns and conditions of light are similar, and many plants are common to both ranges. Both are the product of tectonic and volcanic geologic activity, but this is where the similitude ends.

My first forays to the Owens Valley on the eastern slope of the Sierra Nevada (which means "snowy range" in Spanish) revealed to me the greatest visual transition I had ever seen. The arid environment of this valley is such a contrast

Alpine tarns reflect the unfiltered blue of high altitude sky, Piute Pass

to what lays only a few miles away at higher elevations, the wet alpine domain. The elevation gain of 10,000 feet from the valley at 4,000 feet elevation to Mt. Whitney at over 14,000 feet is quite dramatic. The example here of the contrast in domains so near to one another is a characteristic of the state that I saw elsewhere. In no other state is there such a variation of altitude as you travel from east to west and north to south in California.

My first exploration up and into the alpine domain led to many surprises. As precipitous as the Rockies are in so many of their individual ranges, I was still taken aback by the sheer granite cliffs and palisades of the Sierras. This setting provides a magnificent background to the hundreds of glacially carved bowls called cirques that are home to thousands of pristine alpine lakes called tarns. As you travel up the drainages of the creeks, you step from one shelf to another, with a new setting and scenery being exposed at each level.

Some of these shelves contain lakes and others do not, but in summer they all boast great displays of wildflowers. Shooting-star are very common throughout the Sierra, as are Indian paintbrush and hundreds of other varieties of flowering plants. The slow melting snows, from what is usually a very intense winter with great depths accumulated, feed life through the summer and fall. The afternoon showers, sometimes a daily event, also insure the fecundity of life at these high altitudes.

Though I felt very comfortable hiking the backcountry of the Sierra Nevada, I, too, went my way with a respect for just how unique they are to any other North American range of mountains. My two years exploring the valleys and plains around the Sierra gave me an interesting perspective of this awesome geologic formation. What follows is a photographic and written essay of a few of my experiences during this period of my life.

John Fielder

Morning sun backlights a dew-laden landscape, near Ebbets Pass

Beneath me here I think you'll sit
Remove your pack and stay a bit
The hike's been long and steep I know
Relax beneath my boughs — don't go

Juniper, Toiyabe National Forest

Across the way they look so dry
Not much rain they probably get
But evening showers are made on high
These alpine lands are lush and wet

The Owens Valley and the Sierra Nevada,
from the White Mountains

Overleaf: Sun cups of August, Mono Pass

Long ago it was tall and proud
It reached an age 'twas not allowed
Though life is gone there's much to see
Such colors now in this great tree

Dead juniper, Toiyabe National Forest

Alone they stand against the cold
Would men like us be so bold
To take this test I don't believe
Without a coat or any leaves

Quaking aspen trees, Toiyabe National Forest

Beneath the top of Minarets
Does lay a rock and I surmise
The sun is something it won't get
Until the orb begins to rise

Clyde Minaret, Ansel Adams Wilderness

Overleaf: The Sierra Nevada from the
Owens River Valley

I guess the name's appropriate
At morning look what we do get
Such shadows all along its way
Though they won't last throughout the day

Shadow Creek, Ansel Adams Wilderness

Though beauty comes throughout the year
In Spring and Summer such color here
In Winter they mostly disappear
For lack of joy I do not fear

Around Mono Lake, Mono County

The day is dank, the clouds have come
You just might think I'll have no fun
But when the light is cool and subtle
I'll make great images of this puddle

Yosemite National Park

Overleaf: Owl-clover colors the landscape,
Yosemite National Park

Way up high there stands a lake
Above the rest did someone make
A place I've never seen so fine
It truly is a lake divine

Cecile Lake, Ansel Adams Wilderness

In all my life I've never seen
Such trees so tall and thick I mean
It must have taken years of time
To make such stately trees of pine

Pines, Sonora Pass

Overleaf: Alpine tarn, Ansel Adams Wilderness

Right here it looks a little dry
But look at all this water fly
Curious I am I can't deny
Just what is happening up on high

South Fork of the Kings River, Kings
Canyon National Park

So if you've never had a drink
From snowmelt up along the brink
Of what is one of our great ranges
The taste is great, it never changes

Mountain snowmelt below Mt. Humphries

Not far below the peaks we see
Land so dry there's hardly a tree
How can peaks so close be wet
And of this place does rain forget

The Owens Valley, Inyo County

It's left the tops of all those peaks
And now flat land it goes to seek
Once fast to nothing did it yield
Its future is to flow through fields

Shadow Creek, Ansel Adams Wilderness

One day in fall I made a walk
This time of year it never snows
But where I'd thought I'd be quite warm
I came across a late fall storm

Aspen trees under snow, Toiyabe
National Forest

Overleaf: The Sierra Nevada from the
Owens River Valley

I've seen the tree they call redwood
No taller trees have ever stood
But then I went to this great place
Illusions did these trees erase

Giant sequoia, Sequoia National Park

So cold and blue it makes its way
Through miles of canyon every day
To nothing will it ever yield
Until it dries up in some field

The West Walker River, Mono County

My favorite flower on alpine land
Which in July does usually stand
Alongside creeks and some small lakes
Great color does the wetness make

Shooting-star wildflowers, along the
North Fork Big Pine Creek

It won't be long before the cold
Just takes this creek in such a hold
That for five months it won't let go
Before it then again will flow

Early winter, Eldorado National Forest

The summer's wet, for here you see
Enough snowmelt to sink a tree
And now here comes a summer storm
More water for this place I warn

Tuolumne Meadows, Yosemite National Park

Overleaf: Owens Lake bed and the
Sierra Nevada